Interpreting Your DNA Test

By

Susan Devine Napoli

To: Those who wonder.

Contents

***

Introduction

Your DNA Test results. You in expressed in numbers and percentages. Kinda cold for many to snuggle up to. 'Numbers people' love this. It delights. It excites. Really it does. To look at it closely and dive into the data, spending hours reading the story, a story in numbers.

Hard to believe isn't it?

When was lunch?

As a retired educator of both very young children and community college students, I used data to report success and interpret the research that is also expressed in numbers, percentages, comparisons, and graphs...to name a few. I found it was like another language to learn... a lot like a code. A hard to figure out the puzzle when you are just learning to interpret it. A code with a message in it. The message is you and more you than you may know about. It is amazing what science can do.

I found that many adults like something that conveys warmth and see the numbers as cold. Maybe hoping for a story like this...

'Welcome to your DNA results! You are amazing and we are excited to tell you that this will answer all the questions you have about you...'

It is surprising how close to that you can get.

Really. It could change how you see yourself, which in turn can cause you tweak your life. A better you. If you take it that far.

I found expectations like that in the classroom. What the program did was provide background information: history, research, stories from those in the field. What I had to bring to the learning was...

Warmth. Encouragement. Directions.

Then people were interested. They found themselves a place in education. A sense of belonging. Help to succeed. Pride in who they were that could make a difference.

The DNA test DOES have history of your ancestors in code that is matched with places in the world. It tells you where they lived.

Big deal.

It is a big deal, like walking into a friend's home. You can tell a lot about people by what they have in their home.

The DNA test *is your* home.

Welcome home.

Open the door. Come on in.

Family History Finds

Fascinating what science can uncover. It is the human condition in your family the last four generations or so. Genealogists recommend you do your family history first. Yikes! A romp through birth and death certificates and many other documents to understand your family history, including oral history and family legends. Sounds long. It is for some.

It helped me to know why I am 10% French. And that this history has 'Fils de Roi', the kings daughters, a group of women sent to Quebec by the king expressly to marry and have French babies. I read about these women and who they were. It helped me to see why the history stopped...because it went back to France. It also helped me to see that I might be a descendant.

I am possibly related to one of these women more that the others as I can find her on other people's family history and they found the same answer. Yet, at 10% she could come from the south of France and/or the Basque region, not Normandy like I was told in oral history. These women were not poor as the legend says but women that were chosen by a group of people as more than acceptable. The south of France draws the successful and others as a place to rest. I do not yet know if I am in the direct line but in the bigger cluster.

Wait...How did I do that?

Let me give you a guide to a 'quick search', so to speak. As looking at documents can raise more questions than answers.

Quick Search:

Get copies of all family documents that your family has including any family stories that have been compiled by family members.

Get the oral history of the family.

Look at locations of where the family members lived including: local history and travel information about the region.

Your story is found in the associations with other people, called their *cluster*. These are friends, family, and neighbors. These are the people that live in the same neighborhood, they are on the same page as your ancestors in the census many times. I have found family members that appeared 'missing' living next door or a few doors down.

(For a complete list of what to gather, see 'Research Ideas' and 'Sources and Genealogical Documentation' in the back of this book.)

This will give you a rough idea of what you might find in your DNA test data. These small tidbits of information may be something to look at closer to when the results come in.

Another example is that I am 10% Italian. One family member had married an Italian woman, an immigrant. She was not really part of the family history but her husband was. Finding her was easy knowing his name. Yet my surname is not there in the family finder test. If I am related to her, it is through another connection that I did not find. Discouraged, I looked up the region in the DNA Test and found Sardinia. There is a lot about Sardinia in travel material. Did I find her? No. Knowing the region helped me to see things I like that I could see if I traveled there. Something familiar and in my life already. Sardinia is a Blue Zone, one of the healthiest places to live on earth. I felt encouraged that my good health could be from there. Not proven but it was inspiration I was looking for. I felt like I found something valuable to me, whether I am related to the Italian wife or not.

I did not set out to find famous people or places. I just wanted to know more about myself, as child and a person of many questions, by getting my DNA test done.

There were also a few big surprises that weren't in the family history at all. Results in India at 9.3%. Really stumped, I talked to a hotel desk clerk about receiving my DNA Results who was from India. She was a biology major in college and was fascinated. Did I find out who I was related to? No. But the conversation made her curious too. It was great to have a fellow curious person interested. She wanted to get her test done too sometime.

Even a loose connection like that and travel material showed me my interest in yoga. Something people did not understand. The other big surprise was there were no regions over 18%. My total results are in DNA Test 1, if you are curious.

Maybe there is something to this?

I think there is.

I learned some world history, town history, economics, and found I had tasted food from all the places in my DNA test results...buy accident.

But not really, in my mind.

If you are set on finding something specific, that is harder. It still involves looking at your cluster and finding an association with another familiar family member connected to you. Like a famous person.

If you do not know any of your history, the travel materials can give you quite a lot paired with the local history that most towns are proud to talk about at the historical foundation. You may find names that match your family finder results.

That is a loose connection but valuable and with a name and a birth year, can open the door to people living on a particular street or part of town now deceased, a place to go visit on google maps or in person. Who may be in your DNA test. People do marry the girl next door, you know. Far away places may come from two people in college together, not all that exotic, that had a romance in college. A place people will travel the world to do… get an education.

My connection to Malaysia floored me. I went to an art exhibit and made a necklace that represented me. That was as close as I could get until I learned people come from there that traveled with the circus, part of the oral history. A story of someone who wanted to travel with the circus who recruited from that part of the world. It was connected to me being part of the clowning I did for fun at a church ministry. It was a movie advertisement that brought that to me though the media. Is this the connection, not sure.

It took about a year and a half to find all that, working on it four hours a day. I developed a rhythm to it. As I would go though the list on Ancestry.com at my local library of all the documents they had that seemed plausible. Now I can attend parties and tell stories. I am laughing to myself. It is what a lot of people do with their results, at least that is the impression I get of those near me.

Getting distracted makes it take longer, as something else on the page may make me wander for hours and forget what I came to find, like it does many.

To begin, all you need is a smart phone and a library card, a notebook to write down your 'finds'. It is a little like putting a puzzle together. You are sure to find something you did not know before. It can become a favorite pastime you can't wait to find more.

Take it from me, I feel more like myself than ever before. A beautiful gift I did not expect, that even those who dispute it found a 'different' person before them. I became more of me.

The Map and Percentages

So there it is… a map of the world and percentages of your DNA matched with others that lived there. This is the initial surprise. Where do you begin?

What exactly did you find?

I watched a number of You Tube videos and found reactions from…"I knew that"… to identity confusion. In the midst of all of that were many questions, going unanswered. I found many people not knowing how to interpret their data and dig for the richness it can bring to your life like I did, regardless of the results.

You may have even gotten your DNA Test as a gift. What gift did it give you? It may not at all be clear…until you do some research and find out about the people who came before you. Some of whom you never heard about or met and gave you, you.

These results came though your two parents. Half of it is your father or birth father, the other half is your mother or birth mother. The test shows a general breakdown of the results in the two migration patterns. Though it may not say, one belongs to your mother and the other your father. The family finder test will let you know which one is your mother's side. Those people will be under the 'x-match' list. The others are from your father's side.

It took me a while to figure out that one. The cultures that belong to you can be divided in half and give you an idea of who they were. Here is mine:

Paternal:

Orkney Islands, Western Siberia, Tuva, Sardinia

Maternal:

Scandinavia, south of France, Basque region

I do not know what to do with India, pima county-the Sonoma in central North America or western South America, likely Peru.

This is a big question in the You tube videos.

The family finder test gives me surnames that has most of the French on the maternal side and most of the English surnames on the paternal side. Most of the people that took the test are on the paternal side and English. There are French on both sides but neither surnames from both sides are there. This makes me look further. I cannot find my hospital birth records.

The following are from other writing I have done on my DNA testing and my initial reactions to it. Though not on video, it is in its entirety.

DNA Test 1

Browsing at the drug store I found I could purchase an ancestry DNA test instead of ordering one though the mail. I took the sample with the swabs and dropped it in the mail. I read the comments on the website about others who had taken the test. The comments were divided between those who liked their results and those who thought it to be inaccurate. What is going on?

Those who were happy had done the family history first and loved the additional information. Those who did not were blindsided by the new information and rejected it, of course. Let me propose this: the DNA that was different information than they expected could be the end result of a family history like mine…uh huh…to have to look beyond the oral history to the truth that is hidden.

It is my understanding that a DNA test is an end result of your family history that you hold. It is the answer without the question. The reality as I knew it, was not what happened, not completely. I would have rejected mine too. Most of the people that did not like the results wanted to know the -- who, what, where, why, and how-- an interpretation of the DNA test. A DNA test is really good at yes-no questions like presented on TV: was the killer there? Yes or no. Is the child my baby? Yes or No. An ancestry DNA test is an answer to multiple variables. Multiple incidences that happened over time that resulted in you. You may have unknowingly opened a Pandora's Box of the good and evil in your lineage. One surely to make someone unhappy that you are "poking around" in something they do not want you to or they would have told you. The DNA test can never tell you the details. The records can. Your recollections coupled with the records and the DNA test make a more complete story. A genealogist cannot know these seemingly insignificant memories to guide them, you have to do it yourself.

Interpreting records is not as hard as one would think. What you are looking for is connections between people. Some surely to be found "by accident" while looking for something else. Use this book as a guide to finding your own patterns in your family. They may be similar to mine.

Let me address that some people get multiple DNA tests done from different companies in an effort to get the story. The companies themselves know that there are different results doing this. I think it is because it is relatively new technology and I probably would not get another done. As I wait for my results, I know that if I do get a surprise that I can go back to the records and look some more.

Many of the records I found early on did not make sense until later in my search. The DNA results might shed light on these finds and others, that I did not know were there.

The value of past events informs the present through its repeating patterns. A personal and family history can be used as a guide, just as how history studied in school has patterns and guides leaders. It helps to know it, not only to know yourself better but to feel less tossed around in life.

Based on the family history, my DNA could be:

French Canada

Ireland

Germany

Northern France: Normandy

Southern United Kingdom

Native American: Cherokee

African or West Indies

My actual results are on the next page.

<u>DNA Results: homedna.com</u>

Fennoscandinivia 18.16 % Iceland and Norway

Southern France 15.6%

Orkney Islands 13.2% Scotland

Western Siberia 11.1% Krasnoyarsk Kia

Sardinia 10.8%

Basque Country 10% France and Spain

Tuva South Siberia 9.9% Russian Tuvinian

Southeast India 8.2%

Pima Country- Sonora 1.3%, North Central America, not Inuit and not Greenland

Northern India 1.1%, Dharkars and Khanjars

Western South America 0.1% Peru, Mexico, and North America

Migration Route 1: Scandinavia, France, Orkney Islands

Migration Route 2: Bulgaria, Sarajevo, Bosnia

Haplogroup originates in New Guinea and Indonesia.

I sat back and laughed. Hard. I thought about my Grandma Ida who I discovered was secretly Russian and Jewish. I knew I had a definite connection to her, migration route 2, and even said to look like her. It confirmed that, yes indeed, my hunch was correct. I do have birth mother out there. I too wanted more information.

Both migration routes have some evidence of the religious roots that influenced the families that found their way to America later. Migration route 1 was influenced by the work of Martin Luther, a catholic monk who rejected the teachings and became a reformer of the church. Migration route 2 was influenced by Ba'al Shem Tov, a Jewish rabbi. So much of his life became myth that many were not sure that he was a rabbi or a real person. Someone found his records, a ledger page of where he stayed and that he did not pay for his living arrangement himself but by his religious community supporters.

A second look at the percentages and regions revealed another ordering of my DNA results. Scotland and Norway have a shared history. France and Spain as it was all near the border and have a shared history with Sardinia and the Sonora. I combined both areas of Russia. I combined the Indian and Pakistan. I got a new ordering and an answer to why am I not blonde. I had fewer cultures in me than the original eleven:

France and Spain border has a strong history with Sardinia and the Sonora 40.7%

Scotland and Norway 31.87%

Russia, West and South 21%

India, North and South/Pakistan 9.3%

That leaves the smaller amount to:

Western South America, Peru .01%

There was an amazing amount of island living in remote and cold places. Scandinavian had Greenland and Norway. The Orkney Islands of Scotland. Pima County: the Sonora. This also included mountainous Siberia, almost uninhabited nomadic southern Siberia, and Northern India. This accounted for 43% island living and another 21% for cold climates totaling 64.8%.

The warm coastal climates that attracts people were France and Spain, Sardinia, and South India totaling 44.2%.

This new data gives me clues to why I am an introvert and prefer long periods of time by myself. The extreme climates help me to understand my seemingly extreme taste in things: simple or over the top, with not much middle ground on anything. My curiosity and willingness to explore comes from nomadic South Siberia and everyone else was on the move in these strong paths to north America. My love of fantasy, magical places, and mystery come from the Orkney Islands of Scotland.

India can be paired with the haplo group from New Guinea, a recent location connected to the old. Though the percentage is 9.3%, it does not necessarily mean that it comes from one person. It could come from "sticky segments" that are passed from many generations and not entirely random. Scientists do not know why this happens, until another group of studies paired DNA of the migration to South America to come from Australia. My haplogroup is growing in connections that came to me.

It is likely that India in my results came from my grandma Ida's first marriage and that she lived in Australia. My Dad not knowing his father at all or his family. Now revealed in my DNA. The Devine name a distractor to the truth. There were now two generations of this happening. His and mine.

Someone asked me if I wanted to visit all the places in my DNA, not knowing that there were so many cold and remote places. I said no and shared about the remoteness of the places. I got a quizzical look on that one.

Curious, I went online and looked up all the places in my DNA results to see if I could find something I recognized. I did. Lots of things. Chai tea and yoga from India. My art style influenced by Scandinavia. My love of flowers and perfume from southern France. Walking the local labyrinth with the standing stones like those of the Orkney Islands. When I cook my favorite go-to dish to impress is Pallela from the Basque Country between France and Spain. A pink sand beach in Sardinia. Yes, this is me...

I finally found her.

***

DNA Test 2

I knew I could not sit in a cemetery for days on end hoping to find family that could confirm it, I would take yet another DNA test. The first one measured my ancestry and not anything more. It was enough at that point in the search. Going slowly is a good thing with something like this. I found another test, a Family Finder test on the Family Tree DNA website, especially for connecting blood relatives.

As I waited for the test to be delivered so I could take it, I knew I had found more surnames to recognize in the hoped for results. Maybe this test would reveal some living relatives of these ancestors I had found in the records. The test was specific and would not give a "yes or no" answer but "how much". The amount revealing a possible relationship and how close. I hoped for siblings and cousins. It was both exciting and scary. Maybe I would find out.

I see quite a lot of stories in the news on DNA including Native American tribes that are getting visitors of people with DNA results. It is in 'who you can link yourself to' was the reply type of answer. I have no Native American in me at all and have a link in the records. Many are pondering their results that look like mine and trying to understand it.

Truth always comes to the surface. I love the news feed on my phone that gives me only the stories I am interested in because they snooped at what I was looking at online and gave it to me. I am so glad I have so many others sharing their story who see their truth too and are blindsided by it. There was even a support group for people who had gotten startling results like I had. However, many of their family members told the story that went with the results they got. I was envious.

Considered entertainment by many, DNA testing is now revealing truth that family does not want to admit. What one person gets as results is not truer than another, but it appears that is what is happening.

I sent my sample for the second DNA test, excited and scared. Preparing myself for the results that would come with surprises I was sure. I learned quite a lot from the other test. Namely, that I was not who I was told I was. As I explored the results I discovered that the blindsided feelings went away and I found truth in the results as things I loved were from these areas of the world I had never been or had mysteriously already been there. It included the things I loved to do. Taking that idea further, it helps me to anticipate the results I might get.

The things I loved to do were down played by others and a 'let me show you what is really important to you' attitude. My environment had shaped me to something that was not me, yet it was there playing a lesser role and the things I would run to in times of trouble, my default of activities I loved to do. I anticipate that happening again in my second test.

These would be blood relatives for sure. Though their importance in my life would change. The lesser people become important people. And important people become lesser. As in what already happened with who was my mother. My birth mother pushed to the shadows, who held my DNA and the woman who raised me pushed to the forefront who I anticipated held no DNA like a friend would. There are two people in my parents lives who I called 'aunt' and 'uncle' who were their best friends and was later told, a lot later.

It is the untold that would be in my report. But not exactly the people that scrambled the history but their offspring and grandchild. The females with married names, of course. Another puzzle to sort through. It may not be obvious what I have until I work with it a while. Or acquire greater depth as I go.

This theory comes from my experience with what I learned and does not have to rely on oral history. Oral history could only get me started. In this instance, it sent me down many paths that turned out to be quite different than told. I wondered about who these people I knew really were…cousins, aunts, and uncles who never attempted to have a relationship with me. Little me puzzled and wondering what was 'wrong with me' to not have connection with 'family'. Some refused to play act as others blatantly were. The behavior is clear, they weren't.

Adoption is a beautiful thing. It gives other people a chance to become parents who cannot have their own children physically. They get to have the roles and responsibilities in the lives of a child. Many times, an inner promise fulfilled. The child told both stories…of their history and the story of their forever family. What happened to me was not adoption in this sense of the word. I am still not sure what it was, as I am my father's daughter. Or someone very closely related to him.

People who I share even part of the story want me to give credit to the people who raised me, assuming it was a warm and loving home like they had. That I should give tribute to this couple. That is where I end the conversation. They assumed was adoption when it was not.

it I was somehow moved from one family to the other, and still have memories of some really uneasy and frightening feelings. Afraid that family would move without me for my entire childhood. As I find the story, something calms in me. I await the second DNA test results with hope of people to meet.

I got my results three weeks early, quite a surprise. I looked at the list and found my cousin that was adopted out at birth and reunited with his birth family that included me, about ten years ago at the top of my list. It hit me rather funny that no one else was there I knew, just us who were on the fringes of family for reasons unknown. His results indicated that he is not a first cousin or a second cousin but a first cousin once removed.

There was also a column that indicated the lineage these people came from that included places and surnames in their family. With well over 2,000 people I shortened the task and entered all the surnames from the history I had uncovered I could think of in the search box. As I did I went through those results related to the surnames. What it turned out to be was that all the surnames in this book were among my blood relatives. Every. One. I teared up realizing I got Emilie back, I admire her so much, and all the others too. But distant.

I looked at the ancestry results and it appeared different, like people have been complaining about losing heritage and gaining it back. It was clear to me, as someone who knows a thing or two about research and data, that both times I got different pieces of the same puzzle... reinforcing each other and giving it greater depth. It is how one uses multiple resources. None of the places were new. Some missing places were that way because this database did not include data from foreign countries and they said so. Those places I had found in the records and now include Germany, England, Sweden, and the places of close proximity I spoke about earlier.

I wondered if the database with my DNA was part of a larger database. Could one DNA test be found related to others by testing with just one company? I looked that up and it appears the answer is yes and no. The databases were never put together for recreational purposes but curious people like myself do add to the databases through genealogy and helpful in professions that need it. It makes one feel accomplished to work on and solve even part of such a large and complicated puzzle as ancestry.

Since there is no one large data based that these tests deposit results into, the results vary depending on who contributed to it. My first test is available in drug stores so they get a more varied population than those who would order one. The test goes on sale sometimes too, making it more available to those who think they cannot afford it. As people contribute to the data base, others who contribute later make the results more specific and seemingly change the heritage. The heritage does not change of a specific person, what changes is the information to find out.

Another thing DNA tests reveal is ancestors behaving badly and covering it up with stories of their true heritage that is passed down and around in families. No one wanting to admit a child got born in circumstances they wanted to hide...double lives and the like. As for intermarriage with cousins, there were many people surprised they married a cousin on the you tube videos. It makes sense really, like always attracts like and the fact that genealogists will tell you that after immediate family, everyone is a cousin.

When working with multiple resources as people do when having more than one test done, it is necessary to not throw out the results from the first or other tests. You are most definitely all of what they found, no matter how many tests you take. It is the percentage changing that bothers people the most, who have not worked with multiple resources before. The biggest surprises come to those who have had their true heritage covered up. After one gets DNA information the next step is to go to the records and find out who. Then by using cluster genealogy one can build a picture of the circumstances of what happened. It is amazing how close I got to the truth this way and not only stunned the heck out of family but found I felt better when I knew myself.

My results are as follows:

98% European

2% British Isles

Less than 2% Finland

Less than 1% Oceana (Central South Asia)

It is the percentages that bother people but put together with the first results there is considerable overlap and proximity. Oceana is not actually a trace but connected to India. The first test more detailed than the second in this instance.

As for the Ancient Origins, I gained further knowledge on my earliest roots:

48% farmer

42% hunter gatherer

11% metal age invader

No percentages were given for but also included corded wear and linear pottery cultures. This sounds like a lesson in anthropology. It also includes places that I mentioned earlier: Sweden, Germany, and the border between Austria and Italy, Hungary, and Russia. There were no country boundaries that exist today during that time. Close proximity counts as people never really do stay in one place for thousands of years. Their ancestors moved the families slowly for lots of reasons.

The surprise results in this second test was the introduction of three new surnames with high frequency in my results. It was clear evidence that the truth was scrambled with the lesser actually being more and the greater actually being less. In both DNA results. Chances are looking better as being related to the Fils de Roi, the King's daughters of New France.

I begin with the one clue I have, my first cousin once removed on the top of the list, who we both share an ancestor, Joyce White who was married to Richard Devine. Someone I knew as an aunt. She was not just an aunt who chain smoked, laughed loudly, and loved the outdoors. I can't recall ever having a conversation with her. She played a much larger role in my family history than I ever knew. Why not Richard? Because he is not closely related, the blood relatives are too few and too distant among the Devines. Things are not looking good about me being related to my Dad either, a brother to Richard.

 Joyce has my cousin related to her, a son, and a found birth record that exposed his relation to the family about ten years ago.

I am living in a world of cousins. My immediate family unknown to me at this time. The people I do know are related and cousins from the third to fifth generations and removed cousins in those generations too. Included both on the maternal side are the people I know as my mom's family and my dad's family. They themselves, the couple who raised me, are possible cousins.

I looked in the census records for the man I thought was my father, a name on a postcard, and found an unknown name for a familiar place. Ellington Field, now an airport that is also an Airforce Base near there that had a different name and purpose. The 1930 US census showed a community of some kind near there, Genoa, with the surname of my possible birth father.

***

Curious Cousins

The surname search that is part of my DNA results was a most useful tool. It helped me to verify what is in this book.

I have no evidence of being related to:

The name of my Dad's real father was listed as Raphael Cervantes in the 1930 census of Springfield, MA. He was a student at American International College there. John Devine Jr would attend that college too by accident or design and thought to be my Dad. Something my DNA evidence did not give me, there were no more Hispanic origins in me at all in this test. The prior test would say .01% far less than it would take to be a father or even a grandfather. They weren't. The name would not even be recalled correctly but changed from Cervantes to Cabrera, as often happens when the truth is scrambled.

Devers family, are no relation to me as my grandmother's cousin Ida to Leo.

De la Guipiere and Cloette in the written family history are spouses not part of the lineage. De la Guipiere was a second wife to Jean de Rainville. Cloette did not have any children.

Handrahan was said to be the grandmother to my Dad. She is not related at all. The connection to De Guise is weak, also not grandparents to my Dad. Mc Carthy, Caliri, Rocheford, are all surnames of women that married into the Devine family and presumed to be his aunts to the Devine uncles. The surname Phaneuf is no relation to me either and presumed to be the married name of my grandmother's sister Alba, she is not. They are no relation to me. Vadnais, a surname by marriage to my Dad's brother is also not related to me. Hike, a surname of the author of the Devine family history is not related to me either.

The connection extremely weak because my Dad was not a Devine and presumed he was. He was from his mother's first relationship before marrying into the Devine family when he was very young and never knew it. His files full of information about these people who supported him and gave him a history. He complained of never fitting in, a sure sign that something was not right.

I do have a weak connections to:

Lambert and Fournier were indeed buddies in business and family. The cM in the 50s for them both. Fitzpatick left at some point at 33 cM.

Martin and LaVallee lineage make me a cousin of the Fils de Roi, a King's Daughter and all the other surnames in the written family history back to Badeau and the Belanger family.

Nugent family is also my lineage connected to Wells family not the Devine Family, a mystery surname in my Dad's file at 39cM through two people and 43 cM through one person, and 26 cM through another. So is the Chamberlin surname, a connection with my Dad's sister but weak at 39 cM. Both going back further than my more recent history to Mary Ann Nugent.

I have a connection to the Levine family as fourth cousins, making it possible to be the descendent of Harry Levine though my Grandmother Ida.

My connection to my new cousin is reinforced by another second cousin of the Conrad family. His Dad may not be Richard but someone else in the Conrad family. His mom from the White Family, as so am I. Our relationship to the Devine family is weak at with the closest being a 3rd-5th cousin.

I am related to the woman who raised me through the Beauregard family and one of her children. She is in fact a third cousin to remote cousin to me. I know this because she would not get a DNA test to prove it. The numbers are too low for her lineage to be mine. Rainville at 46cM and Beauregard at 61 cM. We share Marie Beauregard who is also the mother of her father. The surnames of her siblings are not my aunts and uncles all the cM numbers too low in the 30s a shared relative before them, a weak connection.

It is hard to give up these old connections I thought to be stronger.

Surprises

Surnames of people in my lineage that I did not know are plentiful. It is the DNA results of over 2,000 curious cousins that gave me the information that confirmed some of the biggest questions I encountered in the records about family and myself. Curious cousins who I have never met. Curious cousins that wondered what they could find out as I did. Among us are at least four adopted children and a few with no name listed to get their results. They have lots of family they do not know, just like me. It is a strange feeling to see the results of such a test and try to make sense of it. Without surnames, it is near impossible to know except that there is some connection. One needs the records, the oral history, the history of the time periods, the ancestry test, the migration routes, the ancient origins, and personal files of family to get the answer I did. It has been an incredible experience that has set me on solid ground for the first time.

I now know how the past became my present. As I started to look closely at the data in the x-match list, my maternal side. The side I knew the least about. I started to copy down all the surnames I could remember from the known family history. As I went other names came up too. The surnames of many people I attended high school with. Then a second group emerged that floored me...surnames of people in my community, lots of them. They were people I lived among and worked with and for. Professionals in the area I had done business with too. I was stunned.

I am still stunned sometimes about this still, months later. I contacted so many people in the process and none have really told me anything. Some get testy. Others walk away. Still others want me to do something else. To put down the story and get back to something, anything but this.

I know that I have hit a major brick wall.

I wonder.

I wait.

I look through what I have. It makes more sense now as I reread it. Things have come together in unusual ways. I feel good that I know this much. That following a hunch was a good thing.

I know me better.

People look at me...there she goes.

The one that knows herself.

I have a new walk. I am more confident. Knowing part of my own history helps me to see that it is true.

About me.

Something I have always wanted.

Tests That 'Change'

How the data is manipulated has nothing to do with your DNA make up but who else got the testing done. I have watched my testing and people were doing weird things:

Changing their name

Hiding their profile

Getting people that not closely related to get a test done.

Getting people that are closely related NOT get tested.

This can make it impossible to find family and who you are related to.

***

Watching the New Tests Come In

As the months passed, I watched the new tests come in and people closest to me up load family trees. I even looked at every family three available in my second cousin group.

Research Ideas

Grouping surnames by separating the maternal and paternal sides, not only using the migration patterns but the surnames of individuals found in the data. I took the surnames and grouped them using the information in the DNA related surnames they give for each individual. For example: the Fils de Roi, Kings Daughters surname related to me is LaValle. That over time is also a Martin, Landry, or Hus.

To prove a close relative, they need to have a high cM number. Many of the people I was told I was close to had too low a number. Low on the list and did not share a great grand-parent as a second cousin.

Grouping regions. Look at old maps to see possible seaports of how groups of people traveled back and forth before today's boundaries were formed.

Finding lost settlements on old maps. The surnames on them are the land owners and can be compared from year to year watching the movement of landownership over time. Who stays and flourishes, who leaves and where they go.

Looking at You Tube videos of people with DNA results similar to yours. Sometimes only two parts of the world the same but more would be a closer match like it was to a university student that we shared five parts of the world. Sam Ford from the UK. I wrote him an email and he loved the idea of having a match in America.

Visiting local museums, libraries, church libraries. These hold information that matches you to your history and interests. The librarians there have research ideas and stories that relate to a culture you did not know you had. One such visit ended up not being a cultural tip at all but identified information found in s photo. Also about church directories that have newsletters in them. Which later lead to community newsletters found bound in a library and directories online.

Making a timeline of where people lived.

Searching surnames on Family finder. Of the 3013 matches I found one surname match with 1885 people.

Research yourself with your name and birth year in the Public Records and city directories of where you lived.

Group second cousins by cM numbers and identify the x— match to divide sides of the family to find parents.

Read local histories, especially those in your locale and sold widely elsewhere. Especially local happenings that many people experienced like economic or weather events.

Look at local antique shops for merchandise of yesteryear that contain local history.

Sort the surnames by ones you are familiar with in your life, you neighbor may be your brother. Do this in all locations you have lived in. Go to the local cemeteries, look at the surnames on the headstones to find people who have passed that could have been family you never met or heard of. Look at who people are buried next to.

Look through the surnames of people who have supported you over the years with care, attention, even money. These may hold clues to being family members not just a friend or someone who is interested in you. They could also be family.

Once you have the local history learned, go look at signs for streets and businesses to compare with your DNA matches. You may have found your hometown instead of the one you thought was it.

 I did not go look at microfilm, it is too long a process or old newspapers, interviews or conversations collecting oral histories.

***

Making Your Finds Searchable

It is often said that researching family history can take years into decades. People gathering slowly and piecing it together, coming away from it feeling better. Technology speeds it up tremendously.

The process can involve a lot of paper and making copies that are often carried in plastic file containers. I have seen people at a family history workshop with them. After the workshop I went to a library. I was ready to work but she did not see any bins and asked about where my work was. I showed her the two travel drives in my hand I had in my purse. She looked flabbergasted.

People are often afraid of losing their work and not familiar at how easy it can be to digitize their own work. A way of having two copies or more of the whole collection. One even for the smallest size safety deposit box, for the future generations. Let me describe some ways you can save your work:

Take photos of photos. Use digital camera and take the photos. *Delete blurry photos.* Remove the disk from the camera and place it in the slot of your computer. Libraries have devices that can take various sizes of disks and the process is the same. Download them to your home computer. Open each photo and *rename the photo. Make a folder* and name it. *Drag and drop the photos* in to the folder or multiple folders. You can place *folders inside of folders* so your desktop is not too busy. Need help? Local librarians are amazing at teaching this. Use the italicized phrases above to ask how. Sometimes the problem is not what you want to do but how you ask. You can do the same with documents.

Some people have a scanner at home to save documents. They have a scanner at the library already connected to a computer. I find that scanning takes a long time for the image to be made and I don't scan much anymore. It is too easy to have blurry and partial copies as each document is *hand set* and it is hard to check them.

<u>Storing in a Word Document</u>. Name and save a *word document* and then *save it to the flash drive* by drag and dropping it on to the flash drive window. You will have to *make the window smaller* to do so. Any time you want to save something on to the flash drive you can *copy and paste* items into the document and *save* it. To copy click 'control' then 'C' on the computer keyboard. Move the cursor to the new document where you want it click 'control' and 'V'. Then save it.

You can copy and paste from the internet sometimes too, depending on the website.

How you can search your document files and photos is to open the window of the flash drive and open the file. Go to the little magnifying glass icon and click on it opening the search box you can type in. you do not have to remember the name of the file, just any word you want to find in a document. When you type it in the word will appear in yellow highlight in the document, as if highlighted with a marker. It gives the page number to find it and even easier to click the down arrow that will take you right to it. You can search over and over again using different words. It is a process I made up for use with my own work and it is just like surfing the internet.

Many works are copyrighted and are for your personal use only and not for resale. Adding the source to the bottom of each item copied and pasted helps you to go back and look at it again.

<u>Making you finds sharable</u>. It is up to you what you do to share your finds. I kidded about conversation at parties but it could be

much more and become something others will talk about and perhaps treasure.

One thing I did was share my documents with the Family History Library in Salt Lake City, Utah. A way to preserve documents that will eventually be available for free on their website.

The following is all of that research I did for all the writing I did. Though it may not be your family, it contains ideas for sources and my process.

Sources and Genealogical Documentation

Internet Sources:

Ancestry.com, library edition

Heritage Quest. com

Google Maps. Located the location of the catholic churches in Normandy and Great Britain.

1666 Census of New France. Canadian Archives by way of Gail Devers blog.

Kolb, M. "Deliberate Birthspacing in Sweden in the 19th Century"

Kuk. J "Birthspacing in the Netherlands 1820-1885"

Anderson DL and Bean LL (1985) "Birthspacing and Fertility Limitations: a behavorial Analysis of a 19th Century Frontier Population"

Lewis, H 4th Generation on the Robidoux, expansion settlement

Book Sources:

The Normans. .

Napoli, Susan Devine (2009) Taking Care of Susan: how one woman learned to take care of herself

Davis, Alen F. and McCree, Mary Lynn, editors. (1969). Eightly Years at Hull House. Quadrangle Books. Chicago.

Rothman, David and Shiela, advisory editors and Brown, Gene, Editor. (1978). The Family. Series 2, Volume 11 of the Great Contemporary issues series. Articles form the New York Times, Arno Press. NY. Copyrighted articles from 1906-1977.

Herndon, Ruth Walker and Murray, John E. editors. (2009). Children Bound to Labor: The Pauper Apprentice System in Early America. Cornell University Press. Ithica, New York.

Coffman, Teresa. (2013). Using Inquiry in the Classroom: developing creative thinkers and information literate students. Rowman Littlefield Publishers, Inc, New York, New York.

Carspecken, Phil Francis. (1996). Critical Ethnology in Educational Research: a theoretical and practical guide. Routhledge. New York, New York.

Dictionaire Genelogique des Families Canadian, Tanguay 16881700. Baltimore Publishing Co 1967 originally published in Quebec 1871.

Les Canadiens Francais Orifine Des Familles Geneological Publishing Co 1969 origionally published in Quebec, 1914.

Early Notaries of Canada Index. Ruth Ortega Berthelot. Plyanthus New Orleans 1977

The Plantatent Roll of the Blood Royal. Mortimer Perry Volume (intermarriage of royalty on Great Britian, includes Nicolas I

A Dictionary of Jewish Surnames form Galica by Alexander Berder Avontaynus New Jersey 2004 (Discussion on Lithuanian Soviet Socialist Republic).

Back isssues of Family Tree Magazine Missing Matches with Mom May June 2017 p.18

After a Fashion, dating photos using women's fashion trends after WWII May June 2017 p47.

Christenen, Betty. (2011). Girl Scouts: a celebration of 100 trailblazing years. Stewart Tabori Chang, New York, NY.

Genealogical Sources:

Coat of Arm Registration Father Vincent de Rainville, parish Priest of Sommesnil, Lower Seine France 1701

Helene Marie August Gensow, Eastern Prussian Provinces [Poland] b. 1883; death certificate, age 8 Granenz, Germany

Cherokee Rolls: Devine Charles 1/16, James 1/31, Thomas 1/16, James Hernry 1/8, George Otis 1/16

John Devine; Manifest of Aliens employed on a vessel; manifest index; ship mainfests 1930-1945. Also: Leonard Rainville. US Border Crossings 1897-1960.

George Rennie, John Rennie 1940 US Census, Hamilton, Ohio; 1920 US Census North Andover MA

Jules A Chapman, 1861 Census of Canada British Columbia Canada; 1911 Ireland Census (Julie); 1910 US Census; 1940 US Census(Jules E)

Fannie Gaines Butler death certificate; b.1882 d.1944

Jean Baptiste Brouillard 1861 Census of Canada, Canada E, Yamaska; 1921 Census of Canada west Brome Canada; 1888 Sale October 5; 1919 testament Aug 4; 1901 Census of Canada Bangot, Saint Michel, 1991 Census of Canada 3 residences

Joseph Boudin 1901 Census Gaspe Quebec; 1915 New York State Census; 1911 Census of Canada

Emilie Hilab; 1861 Census of Canada, 1850 Census od Canada; 1861 England Census Rodsley, England; 1850 US Census IL; 1871 England Census, 1881 England Census; 1920 US Census MA; 1930 US Census Holyoke MA, 2 residences

Frances Geneaux 1861 Census Canada E. 1895 Notarical Records

Theodore Lambert Hayes; Progressive Men of Minnesota Biographical Sketches of the Leaders in business, politics, and the progression. Library of Congress Printed Material; 1880 US Census Minneapolis MN; 1970 US Census Sauk Spring Green WI; 1900 US Census WI, 1910 US Census MN; 1880 US Census Morrison MN; Social Security Applications and Claims Index; US IRS Tax Assessment Lists 1869-1882; 1891 Census of Canada, St. David pp 88, 83

William Henry Geiz b. 1888 Ditmund, Germany; age22 Warton, MA; 1911 England Census, Portsmouth

Petition of Naturalization 1930

Files de Roi King's Daughters List. La Societies e Filles du Roi et Soldat du Carignan, Inc. filles du roi.org/filles __list, 14 pages.

Berlanger married into the Tache family

Lambert 1659- 1706 Vol 4 pp 110-111. Geneoligical dictionaire du Canada

Rainville, de Rainville 1665-1762 Vol 3 pp349-351. Geneoligical Dictionaire du Canada

Doris Ileen Devine Simpson City Directories 1931 in Salmenea NY, Bristol. CN, Plattsburg NY, Syracruse NY; 1930 US Census Plymouth MA; City Directories 192201937; MA Barnstable, New Bedford, Concord MA, Lowell MA, Chelmsford MA;1920 Census Boston, Fall River MA, Babylon NY, Schenectady NY, Lyndon VT, Rochester NY, Untica NY, Oxford NY, Derry New Hampshire, Avaeo NY, Foxborough MA

DNA Testing Kits:

Ancestry Home Testing kit, purchased at Walgreens.

Family Finder testing kit, purchased online through an article in Family Tree Magazine.

Other Sources, from the people that raised me:

Files (not found together)

A file of collected documents of relatives and hand drawn family trees.

A file of photographs of himself as a young man, with young women, and several photos of babies.

A file of photographs of his travels to find the family history, his mother, and his nieces and nephews.

A file of correspondence with relatives he did not know, gathering information on the family history.

A file of the Rainville Family history he gathered.

A planner with an address book of names with addresses or phone numbers.

A scrapbook of correspondence during WWII between Ida Devine and John Devine.

A chronology of family life.

Files of writing including "Bits and Pieces" columns written for the Ashton Gazette.

<u>Files I did not use</u>:

An autobiography titled "In Due Time", unfinished.

Notes and spiral notebook with family trees in it.

Written Rainville Family History pp. 4-17.

A copy of the program from the 1955 Family Reunion in Quebec.

Chronology of the family history that was with the written family history.

A Word about Painful Finds

As I foreshadowed earlier, some people do find painful information in the records. Including me. It can shock and 'rock your world' to find out member of who you thought were some role, are not. It can feel like loss.

One has to make sense of it the best way they can and move forward with the information as an opportunity to grow into a better person. I chose to do that. It confirmed life decisions I made and criticisms made that were not true for me in my life. It made it easier to hold my ground to write, paint, and sew altered couture. Loving the people I want to. Living how I live…slower and more purposeful. I am having a good time in between the uncaring actions of others that have strong feelings to the contrary. I live in a place with security at night. During the day, I do my work and text my man.

I dress bolder and am more open to the joys in life. I do have lots of time to 'stop and smell the flowers', as they say. Eat out. Discover new things at hand. Become a better person because of the experience.

I have had four years of awful activities that lead to my ruin online, financially, and lost clothes, household objects, two sets of furniture, and a car. Kept awake at night. Finding it hard to get quarters for laundry and broken machines. It fell on deaf ears. I went to seek shelter after leaving the noise and confusion of the apartment I had. I could not run away from it…so I walked *back into i*t. To get my life back. I had the theory that it only takes one person to believe in me to make a difference. I found that person. Now I have new friends and aquaintances to the struggle of life.

It was a nightmare that settled in my bones that will always be a part of me. I never realized how judgmental people can be of others until it was aimed at me. It has softened me, though I am quicker to voice my displeasure and rather cautious to do so still.

I looked around at life several years ago and I marveled at how people can do so well. Now I know the opposite is also true.

Because of this situation I experience a full range of emotions, healthier. I can laugh. I can cry. I can get angry. I can be focused on what I love to do. I have also experienced joy and contentment. I am off all former medications. I exercise. I am in love with life again, though cautious and alert, very alert to what is going on around me to my detriment sometimes. It is a quite normal response to what had happened, I have found.

I am compassionate and try not to carry other peoples worries too closely. I renewed my spiritual ties to God with a greater depth. He is closer than I thought and promises that things happen for good. Though it is hard to find the good some days, I do not need medication…just a slower, quieter life.

I am comforted by those who have done the same from people around me who sell their home to travel. The royal family is in the news today, Prince Harry and Megan Markle. I see their faces and joy. I see the old ways leaving their lives because they made a similar choice.

An interesting pattern I found in my family history is… that is mirrors the monarchy that is going through change. That family revered over time and even the most common of people want at least some part of it in their lives. To be special. The pattern of many people going too far in influencing someone else's life. Pressuring them to a life they themselves will not live but benefit from, not always apparent to those being pressured. A 'this is how it goes' outline that makes people angry and leave or get sick. Really sick and hurt unable to walk up fifteen stairs like I had trouble with to get to my apartment. Not a physical problem any longer because I learned and took back control to my life, walking a 5K every day. Quietly, Slowly. Until the 'Queen' in my life blew her temper and I was forced to be 'back' on medication, in therapy to 'fix' what was NOT broken in my new life. I fought it quietly instead of straightforward. I looked in the records and found answers because history was repeating itself, again.

I made some really bad choices during that time too under that much stress, putting my life at risk to get away only to not truly get free that way. At least that is what the therapists said. I knew they were wrong for me. Getting free was only and uber ride away to lunch and checking into a hotel. No one came after me. Now the covert tricks are back and set on ruining every pleasure again. From blocked TV programs to holidays. I have been and continue to be victimized over and over again. This time I do not run. I find their limit on what they do and how far they will go before backing off. I know that self-blame did not get me free. I had to be me to do it. The DNA test gave me the pattern and the knowledge that I am not the only one.

Best wishes on your family history search. May it enrich your life and set you free in ways you cannot imagine.

Susan Devine Napoli